vital colour

Joanna Copestick & Meryl Lloyd

photography by **Tom Leighton**

vital colour

colour themes for every room

RYLAND
PETERS
& SMALL

LONDON NEW YORK

For Brian and John, Hannah, Julia and Rosie

Art Editor Paul Tilby
Project Editor Caroline Davison
Stylist Page Marchese Norman
Location Researcher Nadine Bazar
Location Research Assistant Kate Brunt
Production Manager Meryl Silbert
Project Consultant Karina Garrick
Publishing Director Anne Ryland
Art Director Jacqui Small

First published in Great Britain in 1998
by Ryland Peters & Small
Kirkman House
12–14 Whitfield Street
London W1T 2RP

10 9 8 7 6 5 4 3

ISBN 1 900518 65 1

A catalogue record for this book is available from
the British Library

Printed and bound in China

contents

introduction: why colour? 7

pure colour 8

colour explained 10

black and white 14

natural selection 16

language of colour 18

colour and texture 20

colour and light 22

colour and proportion 26

decorating with colour 30

linen, paper & string 32

chocolate, amber & silver 54

ice-cream, sorbet & biscotti 72

sea, sky & driftwood 86

red wine & roses 106

palettes and paint 122

directory of suppliers 126

acknowledgements 128

introduction: why colour?

'Colour is a basic human need...like fire and water, a raw material, indispensable to life.' *Fernand Léger,* PAINTER

Colour is a universal language. It stimulates the emotions, shapes cultures and forms the background of our world. Talking about colour evokes music, nature and personality traits and, unlike other decorative devices, it has a human dimension which is irresistible. Quite simply, colour can influence mood, create atmosphere and lift the spirits, allowing creativity a safe and sunny outlet.

Colour has never been more accessible. Whereas once we were limited by cost and the availability of pigments and dyes, now colour is everywhere: in vivid tones, gaudy highlights and on an array of surfaces. Colour has gone overboard and this book is a response to the bright colour overload of recent years, examining the nature of colour and asking for a return to the subtle ground. It explains how colours work together and suggests ways of combining warm soft neutrals, rich deep shades and cool strong tones to bring warmth, energy and simple pleasure to a home. Vital Colour is a visual celebration of colours that capture a contemporary mood but can be used in any setting; colours that don't date; and tones that soothe the spirits yet suit the way we live today.

Seeing colour, using it and surrounding yourself with a personal palette that works for you produces a calming backdrop for daily life. Colour is one of life's luxuries. A home suffused with colours that feel right is always a comforting place; rooms become all-embracing and alive with interesting combinations of tone, texture and scale. But you don't have to soak the walls in lurid planes of saturated shades to achieve a sense of colour. Small details will punctuate the space with a sure touch. Curtains, cushions, throws and lamps can be as valid as a whole wall of deep turquoise or emerald green.

To help you with the process of colour selection, the book guides you through some basic lessons in colour theory and explores the fundamentals of colour and light, texture, materials and proportion before dividing into five core colour groups – Linen, Paper and String; Chocolate, Amber and Silver; Ice-Cream, Sorbet and Biscotti; Sea, Sky and Driftwood; and Red Wine and Roses – containing over 25 irresistible colour schemes.

Each colour group in this book started as a collage of favourite images and materials, so start a visual colour diary or dictionary of your own as a source of inspiration. Every time you find a piece of fabric, keep a leaf or flower, or spot a favourite paint chip or magazine image, stick it in a book. Divide the book up into sections such as colour groups, rooms, subjects, places, fabrics or seasons and add to each section over time. It's interesting to build up a picture of what you respond to intuitively and to discover other influences such as advertising and fashion. We have concerned ourselves with pure, plain colour rather than pattern, but gathering images that inspire you is the best way of sparking off ideas. Start your own colour dictionary, decide what colours you love and why you love them, then see what happens.

pure colour

'Colour belongs to our being; maybe each one of us has his own.'   *Le Corbusier*

colour explained

Defining colours and decorating with them is a rewarding experience once you realize what can be achieved using simple shades. Explaining our responses to colour is as much about an emotional reaction as it is an exact science. Discovering what it can do to a room, possessions or clothes goes a long way to working out what makes you feel good.

the power of colour

Consider what it is about your favourite object that moves you. Is it the quality of light on a certain texture; one colour against another opposing colour; or a combination of tones in one colour that makes a perfect picture? Looking, then looking again, is the only way to get a feel for colour and how it works. You may be surprised that a classic combination does nothing for you, while a deep indigo fabric with a chocolate brown accessory may hit the spot. Colour is so personal that one person's purple is another's deep blue.

Colour has always had symbolic significance as well, affecting perception and mood in a striking way. The psychology of colour and why people prefer certain shades is constantly under investigation. Colour gurus such as Johannes Itten, the Bauhaus teacher, and Faber Birren, an academic and colour consultant, enlarged the ideas first explored by Isaac Newton. Faber Birren undertook much research from the 1930s onwards, placing his own interpretation on the colour wheel and influencing the way that human responses to colour were measured. His work led to a much deeper appreciation of the effects of colour on our daily lives. Elements of his research, which included colour preference tests, led advertisers to the realization that certain colours sell products better than others. Clearly, colour is always there, however subliminally, affecting the way we see things.

the colour wheel

Whenever colour is analysed, an explanation of the colour wheel follows close behind. It was Isaac Newton who discovered that white light splits into the colours of the spectrum when shone through a prism. Each part of the spectrum – red, orange, yellow, green, blue, indigo and violet – has its own wavelength. We see colours when different wavelengths are reflected off the surface of an object. For example, a chair looks blue because it absorbs all the wavelengths of light except for blue. Newton devised a colour wheel to explain his findings and this device formed the basis of many variations created by the theorists who followed him. Johannes Itten produced the colour wheel which is most recognizable today. While teaching at the Bauhaus, he used blocks of primary, secondary and tertiary colours to form a wheel and visually represent their circular relationship. Although a convenient way of discussing colour, the wheel can stifle a more spontaneous approach to colour-combining. Bear in mind the theory but don't be too constrained by the implied rules.

The colour wheel works by linking the primary colours of red, blue and yellow with the secondary colours of violet, orange and green and with the tertiary colours. These are created by mixing a primary with its adjacent secondary colour. For instance, lime green can be made by mixing green and yellow. In the traditional colour wheel, there are six tertiary colours – red-purple, red-orange, orange-yellow, yellow-green, blue-green and purple-blue. Most of the colours visible to the

Arranging colours in a wheel
formation shows how one
primary merges into the next
via a series of tonal changes

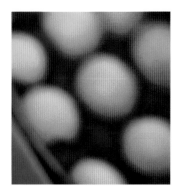

Left **Complementary colours are those that are directly opposite one another on the colour wheel and combinations of complementary colours are always striking, emphasizing the richness of both colours. Here, the vivid tones of fresh oranges are made even stronger when placed against blue tissue paper. The texture of the oranges and the paper also plays a part in the effect.**

human eye can be mixed using the three basic primary colours of red, blue and yellow in different hues and values, but it is not possible to create these colours by mixing together any of the other colours. The human eye is an amazing organ. Under good light, it is capable of discerning up to ten million different colours.

Complementary colours are those which are diametrically opposite on the wheel, such as red and green, blue and orange, and scarlet and lime green. They are the strongest juxtaposition of colour you can achieve because they contrast most powerfully, emphasizing the strongest tones of each other. They can be gloriously uplifting or create a clash, depending on whether you enjoy timid or vivid tones.

Just as important as the colour relationships within the colour wheel is how colours themselves vary. Every colour has different hues and tones which give it a particular colour bias. Certain colours, such as blue, can look more green or purple depending on their depth of hue, whereas orange at one end of its spectrum will actually turn brown. This is why colours that should work together sometimes appear uncomfortable with one another.

Harmonious colours are those which are placed next to one another on the wheel in between two primaries. They often work well together as their natural colour bias is towards the secondary colour of that part of the colour wheel. Harmonious colours that span and include a primary colour such as yellow-orange or yellow and lime green need to be treated with caution as they can be too powerful for the eye when mixed together. When choosing paint, select paint chips

a couple of shades lighter than your perceived finished colour. The paint will invariably look darker over a large area of wall. Always try and experiment with a patch of colour before buying your paint.

mixing colours

You can achieve countless gradations of tone by mixing together differing quantities of the twelve main colours. Mixing two complementary colours together will give a dull grey colour, yet placed side by side they will intensify the other's colour. The degree to which two complementaries become grey when mixed together is known as colour saturation or intensity. In its purest state of maximum saturation, red will be a rich, vibrant scarlet. At the other end of the scale, it becomes much more neutral, as it approaches the dull grey colour at the centre of the wheel, its lowest saturation.

Colour value is often linked to the brightness of a colour. It relates to the amount of lightness or darkness in a colour and can be altered by the addition of black and white. When two colour pigments of an equal intensity, or value, are mixed, the resulting colour is darker, since more wavelengths are absorbed when the values are combined. The process is called subtractive addition, because the light reflected off the surface is subtracted, or reduced, from the colour pigments.

Additive mixing is achieved by combining two shades of primary colours in order to make a third. For instance, blue and yellow make green but the green can be pushed from a vivid lime green to deep apple, depending on the hue and saturation of the original colours.

Left **Lush pink tulips on top of apple green stems shout vitality and richness. Placing a vase of flowers in a room is an easy way of bringing a splash of vibrant colour to an otherwise subdued colour scheme.**
Right **Delicately veined pansies show just how versatile nature is at creating its own vital colour stories that owe nothing to artificiality.**

black
and white

Debates rage over whether black and white are true colours. An object will look black when all the wavelengths of the spectrum are absorbed in its surface and white when all the wavelengths are reflected off the surface. Black and white placed side by side are a classic and complementary partnership, slick, clean and graphic. They are a combination that is at once understated and bold. Just think of black type on white paper, white stars in a night sky, zebra stripes and black and white clothes. The sliding scale between black and white produces shades such as bone, biscuit, grey and steel. Grey is the one absolutely neutral colour. It throws all the other shades into complete balance, neither emphasizing nor enveloping surrounding colours. Grey can also be achieved by mixing together two complementary colours of equal hue. Paint a floor grey and you have a neutral base for decorating. It neither screams out nor detracts from what else you do in the room. Grey also eases the transition from one strong colour to another when placed between them.

Black and white give tonality to specific hues. If you add black to red, the result will be deep brown, whereas white converts red to ever softer shades, graduating from poppy red at one extreme to soft pastel rose pink at the other. When using light hues of a specific colour, make sure that the base pigment is quite a strong tone, otherwise you will end up with a mainly white colour and a hint of pigment, which will look like an insipid pastel.

'cha

White can be used to correct a strong colour that is too deep. As you will know from experience, choosing wall colours from paint charts is notoriously difficult, particularly when there are such a confusing number of different shades presented on one large card. If you find a colour too domineering once you have tried it out on the wall, then add some matt white emulsion to the paint in the can until you achieve a lighter, less aggressive shade. White can also be used to dampen down the impact of strong colours that are already in situ. Used on doors, dado panels, floorboards, fireplace surrounds and woodwork, white will break up and define a room.

Black also works well as a definer in a decorative scheme. When used on picture frames and along picture rails, on cushion piping and skirting boards, it is both graphic and elegant. Much used in the Empire-style rooms of the 18th century, with white as its foil, black is best used in small doses on accessories, furniture and some architectural detailing.

Black and white are useful tools for appreciating the importance of hue in colour. When looking at how one colour, such as blue, graduates from a deep indigo to a pale sky, it helps to imagine a colour chart in black and white to see the difference in colour saturation from one end of the spectrum to the other. Colour is just as much about intensity as it is about shade.

lk, steel, charcoal'

Left **A pile of cushions covered in sensual fabrics, such as leather, suede and rich velvet, hint at the rich variety of tones that exist within the monochrome spectrum. In between brilliant white and midnight black lie a host of subtle shades such as steel-grey, bone and ash.**

natural selection

Textures and colours that occur in nature are often more wondrous than any machine-made fabric or mass-produced material. Think of the multi-shaded scales on a mackerel or trout, the gradations of tone and texture within an oyster shell or the translucent lime green of a cherry tree leaf. Basing a scheme around the neutral palette always produces a calm, unambiguous atmosphere that can be enriched with varying textures and shades of grey, black or white. But nature also produces an abundance of strong colours that combine to give the impression of maybe only one overall colour. A fig, for instance, can appear to be a uniform, muddy, deep purple, but look closely and you will find a rich conglomeration of lime green, bright violet and rich charcoal.

Natural objects are very often the starting point for an entire colour scheme. A collection of pebbles or shells found on the beach and transferred to a glass tank or wooden bowl can define the whole approach to a room. Or maybe the abundance of shades of green

found on the leaves of an artichoke will set off an idea for a space in which the tonal relationships of one colour are explored. Coming at colour from one small piece of the natural world, a scrap of fabric or a fragment of china can be the most successful way of ensuring your personal responses to shade and tone are included in an overall plan. This is where your personalized dictionary of favourite images will prove invaluable. By having a visual record of those elements of the natural world that have inspired and moved you, choosing a colour scheme becomes much easier.

Sometimes un-nameable colours combine to provide a complete sensation. Bread, sugar shards and sea salt can be deeply rich in tonal variation, providing shades and nuances that would take days to evoke using watercolours or oil paints. Imitating colour stories that are inherent in nature is a way of creating schemes that are innately cohesive and credible.

The texture of such objects is another source of decorative inspiration. Matt smooth stones or the elegant contours of a glass bead contrasted with the pitted surface of a walnut or the knotted edge of weathered driftwood provide visual comparisons that make their own drama. Rough and smooth, regular and random tableaux are vital elements in schemes where colour works on a variety of planes and surfaces. In such cases, man-made pattern on fabrics or walls would only be an intrusion into the natural flow of surfaces.

From left to right **Tropical seashells have gnarled and furled edges in shades of white and grey that fold in on themselves rather like stiff parchment; the delicate petals of this pompon-like viburnum flowerhead, which is composed of numerous small flowers, are beautifully and faintly tinged with soft lime; sugar cubes have a rocky texture that throws light back and forth; this anemone has its own natural colour harmony, with its delicate colour combination of sherbet pink with black detailing.**

'The right colours are silent music;
the wrong colours irritate and disturb.'
Louis Cheskin

language of colour

colour and texture

Texture is the secret ingredient that makes colours come alive. In fact, some colours only find their true potential in a happy marriage of hue and material. White linen and black leather, for example, are common associations.

We perceive texture in two ways. We can see effects as light is reflected back from different textures, whether shiny, matt, opaque, translucent, smooth or rough, to be name a few, but we can also enjoy texture physically, when something feels as beautiful as it looks.

Plain ivory drapes are much more satisfying when they have a secret texture. Only by touching do you realize they are made from a heavy washed silk which gives the ivory luminosity and depth. So, the simpler your choices, the more important a role texture can play. Elaborate patterns and complex styling have their own agenda; plain colours and unfussy styles give greater scope to the power of texture.

Creating the right balance between hard and soft textures is the key to generating the right mood for a certain room. An all-white bedroom may need the warming effect of a honey-coloured floor, but the colour can come from glossy wood floorboards, sisal matting, sleek wool carpet, the buff sheen of linoleum, cork or stone. It is getting the mix of textures and colours right that works the magic.

All pictures **Looking at objects rich in texture and tone will help you gauge your preferences when choosing colours. You may return to an old basket or a favourite pair of suede boots. Often it is an object's texture that lends depth to a colour, pushing you in one direction or another.**

colour
and light

This page **Good natural light in plentiful supply is one of the best decorative elements you can have to play around with. This urban industrial building has been converted into an airy and spacious apartment but it barely needs any furniture to complement the fine architectural lines and the graceful shadows within. Successful evening lighting in such a space is a matter of combining several different types and levels of light in order to match the mood of the building. In consequence, halogen, tungsten and fluorescents all have a part to play in a unified scheme.**

The power of light, in all its forms, to transform the quality of any particular colour and space is an impressive decorating tool. Always underestimated, light has the capacity to kill or cure a colour. When choosing colours and fabrics, assemble and study them in natural daylight, at different times of the day and again under the artificial light sources you will use in a room before you decide on the exact shade to use. Some colours, such as light lilac or terracotta, seem to change shades completely with the slightest variation in natural or artificial light.

Bright natural daylight is the truest light with which to work, closely followed by halogen, which most accurately imitates the properties of natural light. Tungsten bulbs have a yellow-orange tinge which affects the coloration of rooms and objects, while fluorescent tubes give off a cold, harsh, bluish tinge. Even natural light varies through the day. Just after dawn the light will be pinkish; at midday the light will be more yellow; while dusk brings a reddish glow. Seasonal variations and geography also strongly affect natural light.

A white ceiling will reflect 10-15 per cent more light than a tint of another colour, so it is important to consider ceilings and floors when adding colour to a room. The decorating norm is to allow the flooring a neutral tint so the eye is not drawn to it. Similarly, a pale ceiling will increase the sense of height and space in a room and allow the eye to concentrate on the walls, the colour and the other decorative elements.

Seasonal differences play a part too. Just as landscapes look dramatically different under a summer sun and an autumn sky, so rooms will vary too. However, the eye has a built-in comparative quality. Even if a dish of red apples looks slightly bluer under one light, the eye will compensate by subtly re-toning the other colours around it so that they harmonize into a new, slightly altered spectrum.

Think about how and when you will use a room before choosing a colour. A living room with good natural light could take a deep shade more easily than a north-facing room where any natural light should be enhanced as much as possible by choosing pale tones of cream or

Above When planning a colour scheme, try different colour swatches on a wall and view them under a variety of light sources. Some colours, such as lilac and red, are transformed by sunlight, tungsten or halogen.

Right Flat colour swatches never reveal their true tonal variations. They show colours but not how they will perform in a room. So, paint small boxes in the colours you want on the walls. They will echo the sense of enclosure in a room and give a truer picture of how planes of light will work. Colours always vary in intensity according to what proportion and where they are applied.

yellow. In a room with few windows, where the light is mainly artificial, choose a colour that always looks good under the bulb. Tungsten bulbs tend to make pale yellows recede into nothing at night, while terracottas can seem orangey, mid-greens assume more of a yellow-green tone and purples look positively brown and muddy. Yellows, greens and creams will lighten and brighten gloomy spaces. A strong red under tungsten light will appear slightly orange while under fluorescent strip lighting red seems more magenta. Under street lighting, which is yellow, it becomes brownish.

Imagine yourself standing on the seashore and examining the play of light on the colours and textures of sea, sand and sky. Imagine watery sunshine filtering through pearly grey clouds; sudden patches of clear blue sky; pale silvery grey foam swirling over sand and pebbles and around your toes; the soft hazy tones of the shore; and how biscuit, beige, grey and slate merge as sand becomes rock. When you think of the seashore, you see tufts of grey-green coastal grass, its spiky dryness blending with the dusty blue of sea holly and the greyish-mauves of candytuft

Despite their continuous popularity, seascape colours can still look as contemporary, vital and uplifting as any others. Soulful colours soothe the nerves and are pure balm for the faded modern spirit. Easy to live with, and always subtle and understated, these cool aquas, greens, greys and blues are at their most pleasing when they are

'The textures and materia sea, sky and vegetation'

'Pure and elemental, the seascape colours are those that surround us naturally every day of our lives'

and thrift, and the austere bone-like beauty of driftwood, sculptural yet raw in its stark angular lines. The colours of the sea can be subtle or strong but are enchanting and easy to work with. They evoke a contemplative mood, soothing, relaxing and wistful, even a little sad. They are the colours of rain and tears.

Pure and elemental, the seascape colours are those that surround us naturally every day of our lives. Earth, stone, grass, sea, sky, tree bark appear to be part of our essential being – so much so that we are always comfortable with them. These colours never fall out of fashion and always have a role in any decorative scheme, acting as a foil for more assertive shades, yet blending with them in a happy harmony of light and shade, strong and weak tones.

'Faded colours – olive, ochre, buff, slate, chalk'

combined with rich, satisfying, natural textures such as soft linens and loose weaves; plain unpatterned fabrics; wood in any natural shade, from pale bleached ash to dark stained oak; and rough jute, hemp and sisal that evoke boats and fishing nets and ropes. Aim to achieve a joyous symphony of quiet tones, muted colours and to create a feeling of effortless relaxation.

Seascape colours bring to mind the pale greys of driftwood which has been worn to metallic silver by sand, sea and sun as well as pebbles, whose inherent faded colours – olive, ochre, buff, slate, chalk, alabaster and sudden surprises of purplish brown or brownish pink – are locked away until a salty splash of sea water reveal their jewelled tones. Imagine the deep, deep sea green of rock pools in the shade of cliffs or the glossy black and amber of seaweed trails floating in the grey-blue waves at the water's edge. Think of the sea on a stormy day – heavy smoke-black skies, the sea a churning mass of Prussian blue and jet, surges of creamy foam tinged with sulphur as the dark waves slap over shiny slate-grey rocks – and you have a colour palette of subtlety, depth and emotion which is far removed from the more obvious turquoises and cyan blues of picture postcards.

From time to time, these cool grey-greens and blues have gained especial favour. The Georgians in Britain used these elegantly restrained colours to great effect on their silks and damasks and they looked very effective on the large expanses of painted panelling and handsome architectural features of the period. Robert Adam, the great

# of sand, stone,

18th-century architect, is closely associated with these particular shades. Newly fashionable wallpapers often featured chinoiserie, *toile de Jouy*, birds and plants. Georgian houses were usually panelled and painted in white lead-based paint tinted with earth colours or soft grey, pea green or sky blue. These colours were combined with unobtrusive putty whites and cool sorbet yellows on walls and furnishings.

The Shakers were fond of a shade of blue called Heavenly Blue, favouring its use on all manner of surfaces and everyday objects, as an aid to contemplation and prayer and as a reminder of their spiritual purity. This deep, deep blue was used historically on the furniture and smaller details in a room to provide emphasis without domination. It is almost at the opposite end of the spectrum from pale duck-egg blue, which is endlessly versatile as a foil for silvery grey, dark chocolate

'Watery sunshine filtering through pearly grey clouds'

The deeper tones of indigo, Prussian blue, deepest aquamarine and charcoal are useful for making a strong colour statement without being overwhelming, while the palest tones of sky, eggshell, dove grey and celadon green are wonderfully elusive and have a delicacy that is unrivalled. Often, people automatically equate blues and greens with strong, overstated Mediterranean colours chosen to stand up to the harsh sun, but these colours are equally successful, and much more restful, if selected from the paler end of the spectrum; they become a tribute to subtlety and restraint.

Decorating with the colours that are found by the sea can very easily degenerate into an exercise in the obvious, leading to a sharp but predictable navy and white or sky blue and white scheme that says no more than the strictly nautical. However, if you choose your seashore scheme carefully, it can become an uplifting mix, revealing the infinite subtleties that result from the textures and materials of sand, stone, sea, sky and vegetation.

Exploit the sand-toned, textural approach still further by using jute for curtains and floors, thick sisal matting on the floor and rope for tie-backs and emphasis, and experiment with hessian, the new textural darling of decorators everywhere – on the walls, for furnishings and even the floors.

'The colours of rain and tears'

'Despite their continuous popularity, seascape colours still look as contemporary, vital and uplifting as any'

brown or silvery, neo-Rococo tones, proving that blue need not be cold, whether richly deep or subtly pale. Combined properly, it can be a warm colour and tackled with tact, a timeless shade that ages well.

Elsewhere, say on the walls, use the quiet sad colours of grey-green, grey-blue and simple pure dove grey for an elusive scheme that does not shout out a statement the moment you walk in a room.

Far left (top) **In a room with such a watery theme, clothes just have to be of a sympathetic colour and texture.**
Far left (bottom) **Shoes arranged in this way suggests organization and readiness for a walk on the beach.**

Left **Delightfully informal and delicately coloured, this bathroom speaks of fresh, clean, coastal living. So effective is the scheme at creating the right atmosphere that you can almost feel the sea air doing you good!**

The seascape colours connect with one another in a fusion of blue skies, grey undertow and sand-tinged coastal plants, suggesting honesty and gutsy tones.

the coastal path

magine yourself sitting on a sand dune, peaking through the grass and looking out to sea. There are forest-green pine trees behind you and miles of sand in front, mottled with water, shells, seaweed and coastal flotsam and jetsam. Look at the colours. You have space and light before you, but more than anything else, you have blue, green, grey, stone and bark, a pleasing coalescence of natural tones that both soothe and disturb, vying for your senses.

The colours in this section are among those that many people feel happiest working with. They are easy to relate to, accessible and make intelligent combinations for informal colour schemes. These rock-pool colours – cool, watery tones, seaweed green, gun-metal grey, indigo blue – don't rely on the sun for their intensity.

Bathrooms cry out for the influences of the coastal path but don't let them become beacons of clichéd blue and white, all starfish and shells. This inviting bathroom speaks of the sea in a quiet controlled manner. Walls of the softest pebble grey give a gentle, almost sad, elegance to the space and a freestanding aquamarine bath is rigged with white canvas sails as a towel rail and shower-curtain support.

Below **A simple turned bowl and a Shaker box echo the wooden furniture.**

Right **Filtering the light with a delicate veil of putty-coloured linen throws shafts of warm** sunlight onto a measured collection of cool, pale blue, glazed ceramics.

Below right **A discreet armoire is useful for storage as well as decoration in a bathroom.**

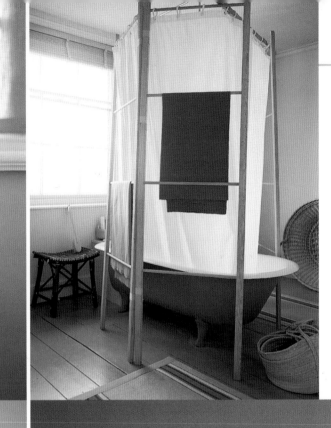

Elsewhere, a linen press stained the colour of pitch and the woven runners of soft, watery blues along the wide wooden floorboards manage to create a nautical feeling without resorting to the obvious. Old shopping baskets and a giant two-handled former log basket deal with the dirty laundry but also invite you to dip your toes into their sand-coloured depths. This is a wonderfully tranquil bathroom to start the day in.

Simple painted furniture, against wall colours that are neither strongly blue nor strongly green but grey-green or grey-blue, is marvellously relaxing and versatile for using as display areas for delicate white porcelain and ceramics that almost look touched by the sea as they show off their lustre in the light.

Above left **The soft rays of sunlight filtering through the blind into this sublimely decorated bathroom are highly evocative of the beautiful light found by the sea. The blind entices the idle onlooker to** glimpse outside to see the **view while also providing some privacy.**
Below **Displaying bowls against delicate multi-hued walls throws them into quiet but noticeable relief.**

Top left **The frames for these pictures are made of stained, bleached or distressed wood and look like the layered and battered patina of driftwood.**

Below left **Peeling paint, vivid hydrangeas and sharp-toned ferns against a grey floor and grey walls bring to mind a relaxing beach cabin.**

Below **A scumbled sand-toned bed base placed against the palest aqua walls and dressed with pure white sheets and a** deep blue-green blanket conjures up images of a hazy day by the sea. Slatted blinds throw prongs of light, like sunbeams, onto the bed. **Top right** Weather-blasted wooden and iron furniture speak of beach huts and a seaworn atmosphere. **Centre and bottom right** Blankets and ceramics with variations of texture and gloss stand out like jewels in the muted overall scheme.

beach retreat

Deeply relaxing, green is a central colour in decorating. Its connection with nature and the sea is maybe one of the reasons people find it so easy to live with. Bathing rooms in plain green, using shades of apple, pea and euphorbia, strong and subtle at the same time, or else using a green that is nearly blue, always warms the walls and lifts the spirits, allowing you stick to plain wooden furniture or painted furniture rather than elaborately upholstered or decorated pieces.

An enriching backdrop for ash, pine and oak, green will also work hard against willow baskets and raffia-seated chairs to create a sense of comfort and warmth. Relaxing and eating will seem the most natural things in the world to do when you are surrounded by such a reassuring range of colours.

Opposite (top left) **Creamy neutrals combine well with pea green and oak.**
Opposite (top centre) **Dressage rosettes provide a splash of complementary red against a green wall.**
Opposite (top right) **Basketware provides grass-like neutrality on a table.**
Opposite (bottom left) and left **Even the brown bread contributes to the overall** colour story of this room and enhances the textural feel of the solid wooden table and honey-coloured floorboards.
Right **A rich orchestration of wooden tones and fragile green walls is a vital and inviting statement. The paint names are as evocative as the effect they create – 'green smoke' on the cupboards, 'mouse's back' on the floor and 'string' on the walls.**

grassland and creek

summer skies

Top left, centre and right
**Cutlery with tortoiseshell
handles; elegant ceramics
that are pebble-like in both
colour and texture; and a
heavy tree-trunk-like table all
recall the outdoors.**
Below **A cushion covered with
unusual brown-grey silk and
decorated with light blue
buttons preserves the peace
in sky blue.**

Below **Sky blue, shades of dove grey and fawn, and pure white create a peaceful retreat to soothe the soul. A sense of quiet order prevails in this serene room that has all the sweet simplicity of a chapel. Light flooding in at the tall undressed windows, a white- painted floor and utilitarian furniture, discreetly murmuring of its past life, could create an austerity that is hard to handle, but cushions in gradations of mocha, taupe and pearly blue with the sheen of watered silk and sublime handmade ceramics, soften the mood.**

Below **Well-chosen books** from the family bookshelf or junk-shop finds such as glass bottles are just as decorative as a personal collection of finely glazed ceramic pots and lavender bags against lightly painted walls.

Above right **Elephant-grey** walls throw a dainty light into a room dominated by off-white walls and woodwork, a richly textured rug and a dark wooden piano – all natural elemental colours.

Georgia O'Keeffe   Art and Letters

ART OF ISLAM T.Burckhardt

country walk

Clean, fresh, invigorating and easy on the senses, pale shades of blue against white, brown and quiet grey are gentle colours to work with in bedrooms, bathrooms and living rooms. Their quiet subtlety quite simply enables you to relax. The trick is to mix dark with light, smooth with textured while keeping your choice of furniture and accessories as simple as possible. Uncluttered, functional but still clearly beautiful is what you should aim for when recreating the colour themes that you see on a country walk. The easiest way to achieve this is by looking at a collection of birds' eggs, dried allium heads or ceramic glazing to set you on your way.

Above left **Bathrooms always work as clean white spaces.**
Bottom centre **A silk bedspread with a central stripe of blue-grey ties a bedroom scheme together.**

Above **Wafer-like edging on a ceramic bowl echoes the speckled surface of eggs.**
Below left **Tall brown glass bottles make elegant vases for allium heads on top of a piano.**

Below **Midnight-blue sofas, huge paintings and chairs in shades of blue are the only colour statements in a pale space.**

Inset **An unusual dark metal sculpture of a dog sits contentedly on kitchen shelves which are painted a deep aquamarine.**

seaside special

n a large loft space where giant, post-Industrial windows shed light in all directions, colour makes a statement on the furniture, built-in cupboards and wall canvases as splashes of hue and tone in an otherwise neutral space. Colour is as much architectural as decorative in a place that couldn't be

further from the sea, yet employs water-inspired colour themes. It is the very neutrality of the background that makes these pieces of furniture stand out, giving them the gravitas and presence of large sculptures.

Top left, centre and bottom **Floor-to-ceiling cupboards and panelling are sprayed a pale eau-de-nil in this bedroom and spacious hallway.**

Below **This kitchen appears to spring almost organically from one wall with a large multi-purpose unit in deep blue and matching chair. The simple wooden floor anchors the colours in place.**

'Reds are powerful and evocative, sensual and symbolic.'

red wine & roses

Red speaks volumes. It is primary, positive and affecting, the visual equivalent of Tchaikovsky's 1812 overture – grand, important, noisy and noticeable. Red is active rather than passive, stimulating rather than relaxing, dramatic rather than underplayed. The colour of flame and passion, red is a statement colour; together with violets and blues, it is more popular in colour preference tests than oranges, yellows and greens. Interestingly, it is the colour most women favour above all others, whereas men will often choose blue as their signature colour.

Even the names we use to describe reds, such as scarlet, vermilion, cardinal, magenta, carmine, crimson lake, Venetian red, rose madder, ruby, garnet, lacquer red and claret, are powerful and evocative, sensual and symbolic. Red is the colour of energy, spirit, power, vigour, love, sexuality, passion and danger. It suggests both love and hate. While its associations extend to romantic red roses and scarlet boudoirs, it has always been connected with evil too, being the colour of the devil and of fire.

Greek and Roman mythology depicted red on the torch of Ceres, the goddess of agriculture, while Bacchus, the god of wine, was often portrayed with a red face. In China, red, not white, is the colour of marriage and for Native American Indians red stands for the desert and for disaster. Think of the rich red walls of Pompeii, Regency stripes and the potent barn-red on the traditional buildings of the American countryside, whose colour comes from the red oxide-based paint made from the indigenous earth of the area. American Federal red is another natural colour, mixed from iron oxide that comes from the earth in rich quantities. Early North American interiors are instantly evoked by simple painted woodwork and furniture, cottons and calicos in homespun weaves, checks, ticking and sprigged prints, almost invariably using these gentle soulful tones and nuances. The natural world contains many different shades of red. Just think of scarlet

poppies, vibrant clusters of raspberries and strawberries, and burgundy grapes as well as the passing flashes on birds such as woodpeckers, parakeets and robins. Sunsets, too, are composed of hundreds of red, orange and violet hues.

You cannot help but react to rooms decorated with vibrant red. The mere presence of the colour is capable of physically accelerating our metabolic rate. It has such an acknowledged affect on blood pressure, increasing the flow of adrenalin and the pulse rate, that many restaurants, fast food chains and dining rooms have long been painted in shades of deep scarlet to enhance the eating experience and take conversation to new heights of erudition. Anyone living with such a vivid colour, however, physically adjusts to their surroundings over a period of time, so that the body ceases to react so strongly to frequent jolts of the colour.

> 'You cannot help but react to rooms decorated with vibrant red'

Red is not for the faint-hearted, but any colour which is so much a part of all the driving forces of our lives should not be excluded completely. People who choose to live with red are often ambitious, with a strong zest for life and a need for excitement. Brave and bold, red will bathe a room with constant warmth, even one that does not receive much natural light. At night, the space becomes cosy with reflected light. Red is wonderful partnered with any neutral colour, from pale beiges and greys through to chocolate browns and black. Red can be very exciting when used tonally with colours that are near to it in the spectrum, where vermilion shades into cinnabar, chestnut and tortoiseshell or crimson melts into damson, deep vine and purple. It also sits well against navy blue, green-blues and grey-blues.

Wherever it is, red makes its presence felt. Although eating areas are the obvious place for it, halls also like a splash of red to create an active sense of welcome. North-facing rooms are positively warmed by such a rich colour, but the bedroom is probably not the most ambient

> 'Wherever it is, red makes its presence felt'

'Red for drama, purple for passion, roses for emotion'

Historically, red has enjoyed huge popularity, from the Tudor period when wall hangings were in vogue to Empire salons, Colonial American farm buildings and Georgian living rooms. By all means, emulate these historical interiors, but try to choose contemporary furniture and fittings to counter the strong period references. This approach does take some skill, but get the mix right and you will have a stunningly effective colour scheme that says much about your strength of character.

space for such stimulating tones, especially when the body craves rest and relaxation. However, it is interesting to note that very young children can only perceive the three primary colours, so red would provide a stimulating environment for a small person. You can also use red in kitchens, living rooms and dining rooms to create a womb-like welcome that embraces visitors and puts them at their ease.

If red seems too strong a colour with which to furnish your home, use it on a small scale, as an accent on architectural details such as cornices, picture rails or skirting boards and on furnishings. It works well in such small doses. The more timid might also like to drench the front door with a couple of coats of rouge red to make a bold welcoming statement or wash one wall with a coat of rich scarlet and let the others languish in its warm reflections. You could also paint doors and woodwork in a strong deep tone or incorporate large window treatments, bold pieces of furniture or painted furniture in rich and vivid shades of crimson, vermilion or scarlet.

Over the centuries, red has been used to symbolize power, wealth and luxury. Indeed, it is at its most seductive on rich fabrics and materials, such as scarlet silk, crimson velvet, deep red leather, claret brocade or burgundy damask. These combinations are undeniably gorgeous, but unless you wish to evoke a Victorian brothel or a sultan's palace, it is perhaps best to temper these materials with plain, simple elements.

'Use red as an accent on architectural details for an instant kick'

Red can also be used to create a host of different moods as well as the utterly luxurious. Just think of how sofas with red upholstery provide instant warmth in a room with neutral walls and floors as well as the freshness and innocent appeal of classic red-and-white gingham and the Eastern extravagance of sheer red muslin.

Purple is another colour that evokes strong reactions. While some adore the rich velvety tones and regal associations of deep purple, others find it insipid, neither blue nor red enough, but something indiscriminate between the two. Purple can be a strong colour, however, imbued as it is with hints of extravagance and luxury. Violet and purple are rarely found in nature, so are all the more distinctive for being less in everyday existence. Strong purple is a definite shade which works well on smaller surfaces in a room – as a bed throw, on curtain fabric, or on a rug or painting, for instance. It is overwhelmingly smart when used for impact against white or cream.

Both red and purple make sense used over one or two surfaces in a room. If you use them with a sense of scale in mind they won't overwhelm the space. Most people unconsciously try to devise colour schemes that strike a balance between calming and stimulating colours, so counteracting strong colour by using diluted tones of each is a good way to embrace red and purple without them engulfing you.

111

Left Use colour to create a specific ethnic look and combine it with a few apposite artefacts for a complete treatment. In this harmonious living room the large scarlet cushions on the chairs echo the warm red of the walls. Even the rich brown of the solid table enhances the feeling of warmth and well-being.

Right A pair of heavy Indian teak cupboards line up for storage duty, topped with equally heavy but sensuous charcoal-black baskets.

east meets west

Rich red is opulent and substantial, imposing and seductive. Use it with confidence on a grand scale, or as obvious highlight, for glamour and gloss.

Deep wine-red walls provide an enclosing warmth that simply cannot be ignored in a large living space. The place demands to be taken seriously, defined well and respectfully complemented. One of the reasons this room works so well visually is because it is defined and highlighted with white and wood. Walls are painted white below dado height and

Right **Making a feature of a piece of embroidered ethnic fabric is the perfect solution for a room with such a strongly exotic atmosphere. It is decoration enough above the pale substantial mantelpiece. A large multi-wicked candle, which resembles a large squat cheese, provides additional flickering light that dances warmly around the smart pristine fireplace.**

Opposite (top) **Cushions are the perfect accessory for completing a colour story, whether they are extending the colour theme or creating a dramatic contrast with the prevailing picture. Here, the cushions harmonize with the wine-red walls.**

Opposite (bottom left) **The studwork on this low coffee table gives a pleasing and interesting texture to an otherwise smooth, streamlined room. The dainty wooden vases filled with small sprigs of red flowers give the room further textural emphasis as well as toning discreetly with the other red elements in the room.**

Opposite (bottom right) **These unusually shaped papier mâché boxes look like exotic fruits of unknown provenance. By choosing unusual artefacts such as these as decoration, the room takes on the air of an exotic bazaar and the sense of adventure is maintained down to the last detail.**

the window frames become extensions of this definition. A plain wooden floor makes for light relief, while white upholstery prevents the space from darkening too much.

A Rajasthani coffee table, African woven baskets and ethnic cupboards distance the space from the English countryside and allow it to hover somewhere between Northern Africa and the rainforests. This is a tribute to global style in an English period setting, complete with a glowing fire for extra flaming tones. Using red on walls is often all that is needed to create a whole colour scheme. You can add furniture and furnishings in the same colour but beware of slipping into overkill. It is better to use wood, preferably stained dark, for a defining edge.

The Georgians loved red, but a different red from this glorious poppy-toned statement in a 250 year-old house. A sharp intake of breath is the initial reaction when faced with such an expanse of dramatic colour but in fact, the senses adjust quite quickly and soon the naturally enclosing panelled walls envelope you with a lush feeling of warmth and security.

Nothing is quite as it seems in such an old house. It is common to find, as here, that the walls do not always quite meet the floors in the expected manner. The cupboards also creek with the slightest movement while the fireplace whistles mysteriously as the wind eddies down the chimney. However, the overall feeling is a vibrant one, despite the Dickensian overtones.

In the living room, bright poppy red is toned down and somehow made more serious with the addition of white, charcoal grey and, of course, black, a positive definer, in a variety of scale and materials. Red and grey are always a smart combination, since the grey stops the red from being loud and outrageous. Pewter, with its matt but reflective surface, can really be appreciated against the strong colour, while black-framed prints sit proud of vivid walls.

defining glory

Above **A cupboard that has been recessed into the wall hides the linen in a colour co-ordinated manner so that the doors can be left open.**

Top right **Black and grey ceramics mixed with Indian weights on a ledge are elegant.**
Centre right **Trying out different reds and greys prior** to painting the room yielded a modern painting trouvé.
Bottom right **Pewter provides just the right tone of grey for decorative plates and cups.**

Far right **The irregular lines of floorboards, wall panelling and mantel shelf work in harmony with the strong red to create a pleasing patchwork of colour.**

purple for passion

Below **Purple is a strong colour and, like red, can frighten people if it is used large-scale. However, the deeply inviting purple of this luxuriant bed throw speaks only of love, not of loathing.**

Opposite (top left) **Calla lilies that are almost black in their** intensity, rather than purple, make a handsome and sumptuous bedside statement.

Opposite (top right) **Purple is often associated with brooding teenage bedrooms. But it can throw off this uneasy reputation if used in muted shades.**

Opposite (bottom left) **The subtle purples and pinks found inside a garlic bulb can provide the inspiration for a decorative scheme.**
Opposite (bottom right) **Purples that are mixed together on a small scale can make rich vivid statements.**

Left **Accessories such as baskets for holding paperwork, magazines or simply general clutter can be used to make decorative statements as well as being useful semi-natural objects for defining a colour scheme.**
Opposite (top left) **Twig chairs with woven raffia seats are given sharp definition with red woollen cushions in a happy mix of materials.**

scarlet definition

Painting your walls with a strong colour such as red may seem overly dramatic but consider the possibilities of using red for sharp relief, as a natural definer or for making one-off colour points. In this sitting room, decorated in modern country style, right down to its twig chairs and baskets, scarlet red creates strong patches of colour that make the room vibrate with vitality. The clever use of natural textures with red makes this space relaxing as well as vivid. The rough edges of raffia, matting and basketry soften the sharp outlines of a scarlet sofa and poppy cushions, making them less jarring. Red always makes an impact, on whatever scale, but here it has a quiet confidence that is quite out of character. Yet for a home on the Welsh border, red is ideal given its connotations with Welsh red flannel and the national costume. Here, geography and culture are good starting points for a scheme.

Opposite (top centre) **A giant, winged, biscuit-coloured linen armchair needs nothing more in the way of decoration than a large scarlet cushion and a loving visitor to disappear into its welcoming folds.**
Opposite (bottom) **In a room that is defined by red, a brown glazed armoire is used to house a striking collection of ceramics in reds, greens and blues. Designed by Janice Tchalenko, they are displayed to good effect on green shelves inside the armoire.**
Far right **A country home is not complete without a delicate sprig of flowers picked from the garden to finish off the space and to bring scent to the room.**

palettes and paint

The colour swatches shown here represent some of the palettes that were used in each of the colour stories in this book. Many of the schemes demonstrate only subtle colour differences that balance together in a quiet harmony. These schemes evoke tone, shade and nuance and prove that, while strictly regimented matching schemes are a thing of the past, colours that really work together produce a harmony that is undeniable. Each colour palette illustrated here is accompanied by page numbers to indicate where you will find images of the decorative schemes and locations that use the colours.

selecting colours

Playing around with shades and colours before you commit them to walls, fabric and furniture is as much a part of decorating as opening a can of paint and applying it to the walls. Choosing the right colours should be a positive process, one that is worth taking time over if you want to avoid the usual chore of painting a whole wall only to discover the colour is wildly different from the perfect picture you are carrying in your head. Getting this preliminary process

pages 38–39 calm, white, neutral

pages 42–43 bleached beauty

pages 44–45 natural linen

pages 52–53 raw silk and cashmere

pages 50–51 classic glamour

pages 60–63 hot chocolate